BEER
BREWING JOURNAL

BEER NAME

Style: _____

Brew Type: ☐ Extract ☐ Extract with Steeped Grain
☐ Partial Mash ☐ All Grain

Beer Story: _____

_____

_____

_____

_____

Desired Flavor and Aromas: _____

_____

_____

Gallons: _____ SRM (Color): _____

OG: _____ IBUs: _____

ABV: _____ Boil Time: _____

Ingredients

Malt/Grains/Sugar (if used)		
Amount	Ingredient	Brand

Extract (if used)

Amount	Ingredient	Brand

Hops

Amount	Variety	Type	AA%	Time in Boil

Type of Water: _____

Water: ☐ Bottled ☐ Distilled/R.O. ☐ Filtered

Water Salts: _____

Other Ingredients

Amount	Ingredient	Add When?

NOTES

NOTES

BEER NAME

Style: _____

Brew Type: ☐ Extract ☐ Extract with Steeped Grain
☐ Partial Mash ☐ All Grain

Beer Story: _____
_____
_____
_____
_____

Desired Flavor and Aromas: _____
_____
_____

Gallons: _____ SRM (Color): _____

OG: _____ IBUs: _____

ABV: _____ Boil Time: _____

Ingredients

Malt/Grains/Sugar (if used)		
Amount	Ingredient	Brand

Extract (if used)

Amount	Ingredient	Brand

Hops

Amount	Variety	Type	AA%	Time in Boil

Type of Water: _____

Water: ☐ Bottled ☐ Distilled/R.O. ☐ Filtered

Water Salts: _____

Other Ingredients

Amount	Ingredient	Add When?

NOTES

NOTES

BEER NAME

Style: _____

Brew Type: ☐ Extract   ☐ Extract with Steeped Grain
            ☐ Partial Mash   ☐ All Grain

Beer Story: _____

_____

_____

_____

_____

Desired Flavor and Aromas: _____

_____

_____

Gallons: _____   SRM (Color): _____

OG: _____   IBUs: _____

ABV: _____   Boil Time: _____ _____

Ingredients

Malt/Grains/Sugar (if used)		
Amount	Ingredient	Brand

Extract (if used)

Amount	Ingredient	Brand

Hops

Amount	Variety	Type	AA%	Time in Boil

Type of Water: _____

Water: ☐ Bottled   ☐ Distilled/R.O.   ☐ Filtered

Water Salts: _____

Other Ingredients

Amount	Ingredient	Add When?

NOTES

NOTES

BEER NAME

Style: _____

Brew Type: ☐ Extract   ☐ Extract with Steeped Grain
            ☐ Partial Mash   ☐ All Grain

Beer Story: _____

_____

_____

_____

_____

Desired Flavor and Aromas: _____

_____

_____

Gallons: _____   SRM (Color): _____

OG: _____   IBUs: _____

ABV: _____   Boil Time: _____

Ingredients

Malt/Grains/Sugar (if used)		
Amount	Ingredient	Brand

Extract (if used)

Amount	Ingredient	Brand

Hops

Amount	Variety	Type	AA%	Time in Boil

Type of Water: _____

Water: ☐ Bottled   ☐ Distilled/R.O.   ☐ Filtered

Water Salts: _____

Other Ingredients

Amount	Ingredient	Add When?

NOTES

NOTES

BEER NAME

Style: _____

Brew Type: ☐ Extract   ☐ Extract with Steeped Grain

           ☐ Partial Mash   ☐ All Grain

Beer Story: _____

_____

_____

_____

_____

Desired Flavor and Aromas: _____

_____

_____

Gallons: _____   SRM (Color): _____

OG: _____   IBUs: _____

ABV: _____   Boil Time: _____

Ingredients

Malt/Grains/Sugar (if used)		
Amount	Ingredient	Brand

Extract (if used)

Amount	Ingredient	Brand

Hops

Amount	Variety	Type	AA%	Time in Boil

Type of Water: _____

Water: ☐ Bottled   ☐ Distilled/R.O.   ☐ Filtered

Water Salts: _____

Other Ingredients

Amount	Ingredient	Add When?

NOTES

NOTES

BEER NAME

Style: _____

Brew Type: ☐ Extract ☐ Extract with Steeped Grain
☐ Partial Mash ☐ All Grain

Beer Story: _____

_____

_____

_____

_____

Desired Flavor and Aromas: _____

_____

_____

Gallons: _____   SRM (Color): _____

OG: _____   IBUs: _____

ABV: _____   Boil Time: _____

Ingredients

Malt/Grains/Sugar (if used)		
Amount	Ingredient	Brand

Extract (if used)

Amount	Ingredient	Brand

Hops

Amount	Variety	Type	AA%	Time in Boil

Type of Water: _____

Water: ☐ Bottled   ☐ Distilled/R.O.   ☐ Filtered

Water Salts: _____

Other Ingredients

Amount	Ingredient	Add When?

NOTES

NOTES

BEER NAME

Style: _____

Brew Type: ☐ Extract   ☐ Extract with Steeped Grain
            ☐ Partial Mash   ☐ All Grain

Beer Story: _____

_____

_____

_____

_____

Desired Flavor and Aromas: _____

_____

_____

Gallons: _____   SRM (Color): _____

OG: _____   IBUs: _____

ABV: _____   Boil Time: _____

Ingredients

Malt/Grains/Sugar (if used)		
Amount	Ingredient	Brand

Extract (if used)

Amount	Ingredient	Brand

Hops

Amount	Variety	Type	AA%	Time in Boil

Type of Water: _____

Water: ☐ Bottled   ☐ Distilled/R.O.   ☐ Filtered

Water Salts: _____

Other Ingredients

Amount	Ingredient	Add When?

NOTES

NOTES

BEER NAME

Style: _____

Brew Type: ☐ Extract   ☐ Extract with Steeped Grain
            ☐ Partial Mash   ☐ All Grain

Beer Story: _____
_____
_____
_____
_____

Desired Flavor and Aromas: _____
_____
_____

Gallons: _____   SRM (Color): _____
OG: _____   IBUs: _____
ABV: _____   Boil Time: _____

Ingredients

Malt/Grains/Sugar (if used)		
Amount	Ingredient	Brand

Extract (if used)

Amount	Ingredient	Brand

Hops

Amount	Variety	Type	AA%	Time in Boil

Type of Water: _____

Water:　　　　□ Bottled　　　□ Distilled/R.O.　　　□ Filtered

Water Salts: _____

Other Ingredients

Amount	Ingredient	Add When?

NOTES

NOTES

BEER NAME

Style: _____

Brew Type: ☐ Extract   ☐ Extract with Steeped Grain
             ☐ Partial Mash   ☐ All Grain

Beer Story: _____
_____
_____
_____
_____

Desired Flavor and Aromas: _____
_____
_____

Gallons: _____   SRM (Color): _____

OG: _____   IBUs: _____

ABV: _____   Boil Time: ___ _____

Ingredients

Malt/Grains/Sugar (if used)		
Amount	Ingredient	Brand

Extract (if used)

Amount	Ingredient	Brand

Hops

Amount	Variety	Type	AA%	Time in Boil

Type of Water: _____

Water: ☐ Bottled   ☐ Distilled/R.O.   ☐ Filtered

Water Salts: _____

Other Ingredients

Amount	Ingredient	Add When?

NOTES

NOTES

BEER NAME

Style: _____

Brew Type: ☐ Extract   ☐ Extract with Steeped Grain
              ☐ Partial Mash   ☐ All Grain

Beer Story: _____

_____

_____

_____

_____

Desired Flavor and Aromas: _____

_____

_____

Gallons: _____   SRM (Color): _____

OG: _____   IBUs: _____

ABV: _____   Boil Time: _____

Ingredients

Malt/Grains/Sugar (if used)		
Amount	Ingredient	Brand

Extract (if used)

Amount	Ingredient	Brand

Hops

Amount	Variety	Type	AA%	Time in Boil

Type of Water: _____

Water: ☐ Bottled   ☐ Distilled/R.O.   ☐ Filtered

Water Salts: _____

Other Ingredients

Amount	Ingredient	Add When?

NOTES

NOTES

BEER NAME

Style: _____

Brew Type: ☐ Extract   ☐ Extract with Steeped Grain
            ☐ Partial Mash ☐ All Grain

Beer Story: _____
_____
_____
_____
_____

Desired Flavor and Aromas: _____
_____
_____

Gallons: _____   SRM (Color): _____

OG: _____   IBUs: _____

ABV: _____   Boil Time: _____

Ingredients

Malt/Grains/Sugar (if used)		
Amount	Ingredient	Brand

Extract (if used)

Amount	Ingredient	Brand

Hops

Amount	Variety	Type	AA%	Time in Boil

Type of Water: _____

Water: ☐ Bottled   ☐ Distilled/R.O.   ☐ Filtered

Water Salts: _____

Other Ingredients

Amount	Ingredient	Add When?

NOTES

NOTES

BEER NAME

Style: _____

Brew Type: ☐ Extract   ☐ Extract with Steeped Grain

                 ☐ Partial Mash   ☐ All Grain

Beer Story: _____

_____

_____

_____

_____

Desired Flavor and Aromas: _____

_____

_____

Gallons: _____   SRM (Color): _____

OG: _____   IBUs: _____

ABV: _____   Boil Time: _____

Ingredients

Malt/Grains/Sugar (if used)		
Amount	Ingredient	Brand

Extract (if used)

Amount	Ingredient	Brand

Hops

Amount	Variety	Type	AA%	Time in Boil

Type of Water: _____

Water: ☐ Bottled ☐ Distilled/R.O. ☐ Filtered

Water Salts: _____

Other Ingredients

Amount	Ingredient	Add When?

NOTES

NOTES

Printed in Germany
by Amazon Distribution
GmbH, Leipzig